OXFORD ENGLISH

QUEST

Y4/P5

PUPIL BOOK 2

KATE RUTTLE

Contents

Look for these icons so you know what to do.

All the activities are colour coded.
You will **all** be able to have a go at the green activities.

Most of you can do the orange activities.

Some of you can do the red activities.

Think it

Think it!

Just because you are quiet when you think, it doesn't mean you're not working! Think about the question carefully, and be ready to talk about your answer. There's often no right or wrong.

Say it

Say it!

For these activities you will need to say your answer, or discuss what you think. Make sure you have thought about what you want to say before you speak. Don't forget to listen too! You will need to work with a friend, or in a small group.

Write it!

For these activities you will need to write things down, so make sure you have a pen or pencil and paper. Before you write, decide whether you need to write in notes, or in your best handwriting.

Enjoy it?

This icon asks you to think whether you have enjoyed what you have read. Think about what you liked – and what you didn't!

Draw it!

For these activities you will need pencils or pens for drawing. Think about the reason for your drawing before you start. Is it to make something look better, or to make something clearer to someone else?

Act it!

This icon tells you that you will need to act these activities. You will need to work with a friend, or in a small group.

p.4–15

This icon tells you which pages in the Companion to look at to answer the question.

This icon tells you helpful things.

Unit 1 Watling Street

Enjoy it?

p.4–17 Did you enjoy reading about Watling Street in unit 1 of the Companion? Which time in history would you choose to travel along Watling Street? Who would you be?

C45 AD

1100 AD

C1200

1836

Think it

Like it?

Ways of presenting information

p.4–17 Look at all the different ways of showing information in unit 1 of the Companion, 'Watling Street'. Which one do you find easiest to use? Why?

Work it out!

What are they saying?

p.4–5 Look at the picture on pages 4 and 5 of the Companion. Find a speech bubble which means the same as:

1 Hail and farewell (in Latin).
2 I will gladly ride with you.
3 We've got a new car!
4 Come this way.
5 How much will it cost to go on your coach?
6 It will cost you one penny to use this road.

In your book, write:

1 = Ave atque vale
2 =

Split it!

Syllable search

p.6–9 **Write these words from pages 6 – 9 of the Companion in syllables, to work out how to pronounce them.**

1 Watling
2 agrimensores
3 camber
4 materials
5 surveyors
6 packhorses
7 pilgrimages
8 Canterbury
9 archbishop
10 Jerusalem

In your book, write:

1. Watling: Wat - ling
2.

Think it

Think it!

Sentence summary

Read each set of sentences. Which sentence – A, B or C – best summarises the information on the topic given in the Companion?

1 p.6–7 **Roman road building**

Is it:

A Roman roads were built by legions because the legions contained Rome's best soldiers.

B Roman roads were built by legions because then the Roman people and goods could get around the country easily.

C Roman roads were built by legions because the agrimensores decided where the road should go.

2 p.6–7 Straight Roman roads

Is it:

A Roman roads were straight because straight roads meant shorter journeys.

B Roman roads were straight because that's how the legions made them.

C Roman roads were straight because the countryside was full of villas.

3 p.8–9 Watling Street in the Middle Ages

Is it:

A Watling Street began to crumble because the new rulers didn't need the roads.

B Watling Street began to crumble because the Romans left Britain.

C Watling Street began to crumble because heavy carts got stuck in the mud.

4 p.8–9 Robbers on Watling Street

Is it:

A Trees and bushes beside the road were cut down so robbers could be hanged there.

B Trees and bushes beside the road were cut down so robbers couldn't hide near the road.

C Trees and bushes beside the road were cut down so people could use packhorses.

Sights, sounds, smells

p.8 **Look at the picture on page 8 of the Companion and imagine you are one of the people in it.**

- Where are you going? Why?
- What can you see?
- What kinds of sounds can you hear?
- What kinds of smells can you smell?
- Are you eating anything? What does it taste like?
- What does the road feel like under your feet?
- Are you happy or frightened? Why?

When you have discussed all these ideas, write a paragraph describing the scene.

Three-part sentence

Join together information in three of these sentences to make one longer three-part sentence. Don't forget to use commas to show the chunks of meaning within the sentence.

Example:
The Romans built Watling Street, which went through Canterbury, and used it for almost 400 years.

The Romans built Watling Street.

Watling Street went through Canterbury.

Watling Street went through London.

Watling Street went to the border of the Empire.

The Romans used Watling Street for almost 400 years.

The Romans left Britain.

The Anglo-Saxons let the road crumble.

The Anglo-Saxons didn't like living in villas.

The Anglo-Saxons didn't use the road much.

Robbers hid near the road.

Robbers wanted to rob the travellers.

Trees were cut down 10 m from the road.

Robbers were sometimes caught.

Robbers were hanged.

Base form of verbs

Read the verbs in each circle. Can you work out what the base form is?

In your book, write:
1 = to build
2 =

Example:

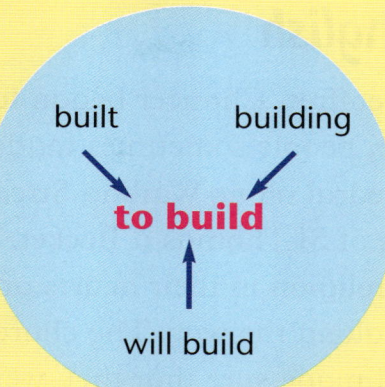

built   building
to build
will build

1

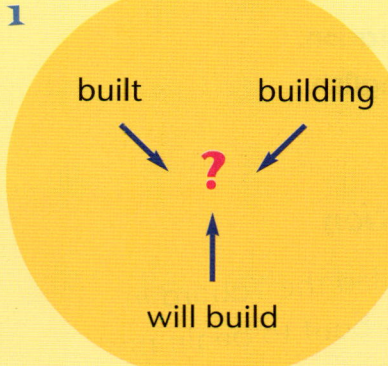

built   building
?
will build

2

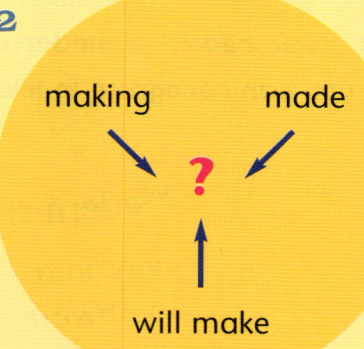

making   made
?
will make

3

marched   will march
?
marching

4

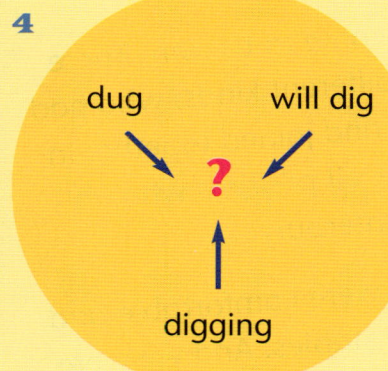

dug   will dig
?
digging

5

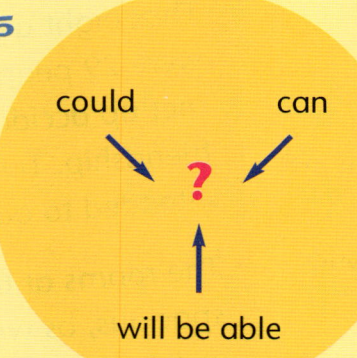

could   can
?
will be able

6

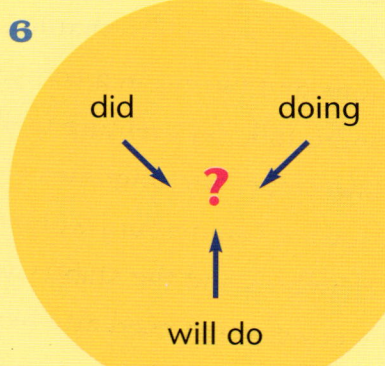

did   doing
?
will do

7

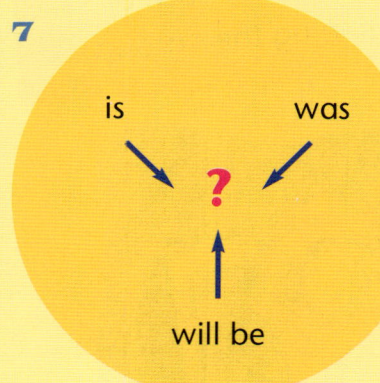

is   was
?
will be

8

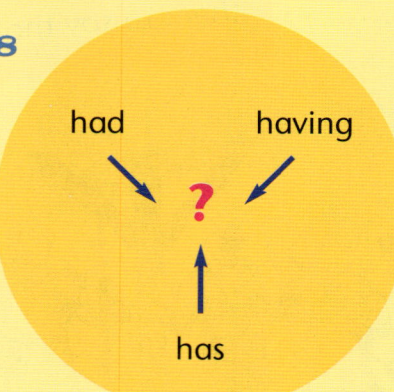

had   having
?
has

Chaucer's English

In about 1386, Geoffrey Chaucer began to write *The Canterbury Tales*. In Chaucer's time, people sometimes made pilgrimages from London to Canterbury Cathedral along Watling Street. They went to the Cathedral to pray at the shrine of St Thomas à Becket. The travellers were meant to go on pilgrimages with religion in their hearts and not to complain if they had to suffer discomfort along the way. The characters in Chaucer's tales were not all very religious and made sure that they were always comfortable and well fed.

Read this part of the introduction to *The Canterbury Tales*, written in Middle English (Chaucer's English). Then read the modern translation. Talk about the words and phrases you can recognise in Middle English.

Middle English

Bifil that in that seson, on a day,
In Southwerk at the Tabard as I lay
Redy to wenden on my pilgrymage
To Caunterbury with ful devout corage,
At nyght was come into that hostelrye
Wel nyne and twenty in a compaignye
Of sondry folk, by aventure yfalle
In felaweshipe, and pilgrimes were they alle,
That toward Caunterbury wolden ryde.
The chambres and the stables weren wyde,
And wel we weren esed atte beste;
And shortly, whan the sonne was to reste,
So hadde I spoken with hem everichon
That I was of hir felaweshipe anon …

Geoffrey Chaucer

Modern translation

I was in an inn called the Tabard in Southwark. I was about to begin my pilgrimage to Canterbury and feeling very religious.

That night a group came to the inn. There were 29 people, of different kinds, who had met up accidentally and joined together in friendship. They were all pilgrims who intended to go to Canterbury.

The rooms at the inn were comfortable and spacious, as were the stables. And we were well looked after. And, by the time the sun had gone down, I had spoken to each of them to say that I was joining their group.

The Nun's Priest's Tale

Read this description of the Nun's Priest's Tale from *The Canterbury Tales*. Draw a cartoon strip to show the main events in the story.

Chanticleer was a proud, but sometimes foolish, rooster. He was married to Pertelote. Night after night, Chanticleer woke Pertelote up by telling her of his bad dreams and asking her what she thought they meant. But Pertelote soon got tired of hearing Chanticleer's dreams. Early one morning, when he wasn't feeling very well, Chanticleer woke Pertelote up and complained that in his dream he had been chased by a fox. Sleepily, Pertelote told him not to worry and said that he should go and look for some herbs to cure his illness. Off went Chanticleer, in search of his herbs, while Pertelote went back to sleep.

A few minutes later, Pertelote heard a strange noise. She looked up and saw a fox running off with his teeth clamped firmly around Chanticleer's middle. Pertelote started clucking and raising such a storm of dirt and feathers that the woman who looked after them came running out to see what the problem was. She started hurling rocks at the fox, who dropped the rooster and ran to safety.

11

Act it!

Hot seating

p.10–11 **Reread pages 10 and 11 of the Companion. Choose one person to be 'hotseated'. That person, decide whether you want to be Shakespeare or Queen Elizabeth I. Everyone else, think of questions you would like to ask the character.**

Questions you could ask are:

Shakespeare:
- Did you join a travelling theatre company?
- Where did you like to perform most? Why?
- What did you feel when people drove you out of town?
- Was the food good?
- What was on the cart you took with you and how did you use everything?
- Were the inns comfortable?

Queen Elizabeth I:
- Why did you travel in the hottest months?
- Did you feel guilty when all your servants had to walk and you drove in your carriage?
- What was in all those carts and packages?
- Did you get bored on the journeys?
- Why did people make such a fuss of you when you went to visit them?

Cunning commas

Think about these four reasons for using commas:

1 to separate items in a list (e.g. *it was a big, dangerous machine*)

2 around additional information (e.g. *George Stephenson's engine, the Rocket, was built in 1829*)

3 to separate different chunks of information (e.g. *Thomas Telford was known as a canal maker, but he also built roads and bridges*)

4 after an expression of time or place (e.g. *At first, running water was used to power factories*)

Rewrite these sentences, adding commas.

1 By the 1850s there were factories in many parts of Britain.

2 Many large busy towns grew up around the factories. Although factory owners were rich the workers were paid very little.

3 Factory workers lived in rows of tiny houses on narrow streets called slums which were often dirty and crowded. Disease spread quickly because the houses of the factory workers had no running water the streets were filthy and the air was full of smoke from the factories.

Summarise it!

Highwaymen

p.8 p.13 **What can you find out about highwaymen? Write a summary of the information you find.**

Use:

⊙ pages 8 and 13 of the Companion;

⊙ verses from the poem *The Highwaymen*;

⊙ ICT and information sources.

Verses from *The Highwaymen*

The wind was a torrent of darkness among the gusty trees,
The moon was a ghostly galleon tossed upon cloudy seas,
The road was a ribbon of moonlight over the purple moor,
And the highwayman came riding –
Riding – riding –
The highwayman came riding up to the old inn-door.
He'd a French cocked-hat on his forehead, a bunch of lace at his chin,
A coat of the claret velvet, and breeches of brown doeskin;
They fitted with never a wrinkle; his boots were up to the thigh!
And he rode with a jewelled twinkle,
His pistol butts a-twinkle,
His rapier hilt a-twinkle, under the jewelled sky.

Alfred Noyes

Powerful verbs

Read these sentences. Write at least five powerful verbs which could take the place of the underlined verb in each sentence and make the meaning clearer.

1 The wheels <u>went</u> over the hard and frosty ground.
2 Mr Pickwick <u>got</u> into his coach.
3 The mud and rain <u>came</u> in through the open windows of the carriage.
4 The horses <u>went</u> down the slippery road.
5 Mr Pickwick <u>went</u> into the inn.

Info search

p.4–17 **Find the information using headings and topic sentences.
Answer the questions in sentences.**

Before Tudor times

1 Why was the arrival of Emperor Claudius and his men important?
2 Why did the Romans stop using Watling Street?
3 When the Romans left Britain, Watling Street was a good road.
   Less than 500 years later, it was crumbling. Why?
4 Why was it difficult for William of Normandy to find men
   to mend the road?
5 Name four towns that Watling Street passes through.
6 Why did the Romans need good roads?

Tudor times and Georgian times

1 Why do you think there were inns for
   travellers along Watling Street in
   Tudor times?
2 What was the royal progress?
3 What was Thomas Telford famous for?
4 Why do you think Telford put
   toll gates on his roads?
5 What do you think a mail coach was?
6 Why was travelling by road
   dangerous in Tudor times and
   Georgian times?

19th and 20th centuries

1 Who was Mr Pickwick?
2 Explain why travelling by coach
   in Victorian times wasn't always
   comfortable.
3 Why do you think there were inns
   for travellers along Watling Street
   in Victorian times?
4 What atmosphere was Charles
   Dickens trying to create in his
   description of the Saracen's
   Head Inn? How did he do it?
5 Why did the government build
   motorways?
6 What do you think should
   happen next to Watling Street?

Enjoy it?

p.18-31 Read through unit 2 of the Companion. Which poems did you enjoy most? Why? Or did you prefer reading the explanations? Why?

Say it

Learn it!

Poem

p.18-31 Choose a poem from unit 2 to learn by heart. Ask if you can recite it to your friends.

Find it!

Looks different – sounds the same

p.18-31 Choose any poem in unit 2 of the Companion. Make lists of words which have the same vowel phonemes (sounds), but look different.

Underline the letter patterns that represent the vowel phoneme that sounds the same.

In your book, write:

Looks different, sounds the same:

r<u>ow</u>s – vi<u>o</u>la

l<u>i</u>nes – v<u>i</u>olins

Talk about it!

Water cycle

Look at this diagram of the water cycle. Can you work out what happens? Start with rain falling on the hills and mountains. Where does the water go? What happens next? Where does the next rain come from?

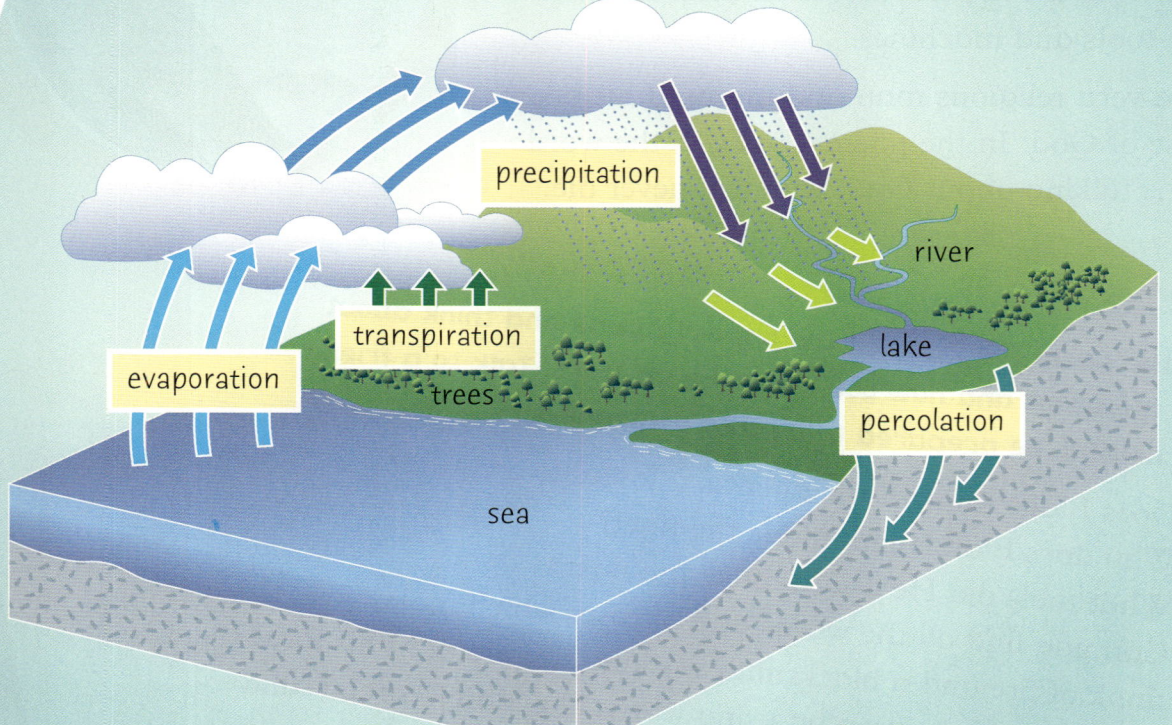

precipitation

river

transpiration

lake

evaporation

trees

percolation

sea

Spell it!

-tion words

Look at all the -tion words in the water cycle diagram. Write them in a list.

How many more -tion words can you find?

Fact

English words do not end –shon. But there are two that end –shion. Can you find them?

Which other spelling patterns can you find that make the sound 'shon' at the end of a word?

Tiger! Tiger!

William Blake

The English poet and artist, William Blake, lived from 1757 to 1827. This was the time of the Industrial Revolution, when huge factories were built to house enormous and noisy machines.

During this time, blacksmiths also worked at their fires, hammering the red hot metal on their anvils to shape it for tools and machines.

Blake was a very religious man and many of his poems are in praise of God. In the poem *The Tiger*, the word 'immortal' is talking about God, who will never die.

Read the poem *The Tiger* on the opposite page and think about these questions and how you know the answers. Talk to a friend if it's helpful. Be prepared to discuss your answers.

1 Does Blake think of the tiger as a loveable creature?
2 Who does Blake think made the tiger?
3 What tools did He use to make the tiger?
4 Can you find all the words and phrases which make you think of fire and a blacksmith working hot metal at his forge?
5 Why does Blake keep on using words like 'dare', 'dread' and 'fearful'?
6 Why is the tiger 'burning bright in the forests of the night'?
7 Why does Blake talk about the tiger as having 'symmetry'?
8 In the fifth verse, the tiger has been finished. Why do you think Blake talks about water in this verse, not fire?
9 What is the difference between the first verse and the last verse? Do you think this was done on purpose?
10 Read the poem again, aloud, and imagine that you are hammering a hot piece of metal while you do so. Can you hear the hammer beats throughout the poem?

The Tiger

Tiger! Tiger! Burning bright
In the forests of the night
What immortal hand or eye
Could frame thy fearful symmetry?

In what distant deeps or skies
Burnt the fire of thine eyes?
On what wings dare he aspire
What the hand dare seize the fire?

And what shoulder and what art
Could twist the sinews of thy heart?
And when thy heart began to beat,
What dread hand, and what dread feet?

What the hammer? What the chain?
In what furnace was thy brain?
What the anvil
What dread grasp
Dare its deadly terrors clasp?

When the stars threw down their spears
And watered heaven with their tears,
Did He smile, His work to see?
Did He who made the lamb make thee?

Tiger! Tiger! Burning bright
In the forests of the night
What immortal hand or eye
Dare frame thy fearful symmetry?

William Blake

Sort it!

Finding examples

Read the poem *The Tiger*. Can you find examples of:

- rhyme – words with the same sound in the final syllable (e.g. *hat*, *sat*);
- half rhyme – words which almost rhyme (e.g. *hen*, *pin*);
- alliteration – a phrase where words begin with the same phoneme (e.g. *six sizzling sausages*);
- assonance – words where vowel sounds are repeated (e.g. *dream team*);
- onomatopoeia – words which sound like their meaning (e.g. *hiss*, *bang*)?

Picture it!

Picture a poem

p.18–31 Choose one of the poems from unit 2, 'Rhyme and Reason', in the Companion. Draw a picture of what the poem describes. Add labels to show all the details you have drawn. Use words and phrases from the poem to make the labels.

Think it

Compare it!

Bird poems

p.21 Read the poem *The Eagle* on page 21 of the Companion, then read *The Hawk* on this page.

Think about similarities and differences in the poems.

Think about:

- the overall effect of the poems;
- how the poems make you feel;
- what the poems tell you about the birds they describe;
- the language used;
- the sounds used;
- the layout.

In your book, write:

Similarities	Differences
theme	only one poem rhymes

The Hawk

Afternoon,
With just enough of a breeze
for him to ride it
lazily, a hawk
sails still-winged
up the slope of a stubble-covered hill,
so low
he nearly
touches his shadow

Robert Sund

Say it

Discuss it!

Bear

p.22 Read the poem *Bear* on page 22 of the Companion.

Is the bear better off in the zoo, or not? Why? Discuss with a partner.

Adapt it!

Jelly instructions

p.24 Read the poem *Making Jelly* on page 24 of the Companion.

If the narrator of the poem were to write instructions for making jelly, what would he write? Write the instructions in your book.

Write it!

Habitats

polar bear

camel

p.22–23 Why would each of these creatures die in the other's habitat?

Compare the creatures, using the information on pages 22 and 23 of the Companion, then write about them. Underline the topic sentences and key words you use in each paragraph.

Move it!

Synonyms

Read all these different ways of moving. Think about what each of the words in the box means. Group the words to show which have the meanings listed below.

1 to move along quickly: *bolt, canter, career, dart, dash, flit*
2 to move along slowly: *amble, crawl, dawdle, drift*
3 to move along gracefully: *dance, flow, glide*
4 to move along awkwardly: *dodder, falter, flounder, lumber*
5 to move along stealthily: *crawl, creep, edge*
6 to move things from one place to another: *carry, export, import*

gallop   hurry   march   nip   race

rush   shake   shuffle   skate   slide

sneak   speed   stagger   stroll   stumble

slip   transport   twist   wiggle   zoom

totter

In your book, write:

1. gallop, hurry,
2. stroll,
3.

Moving

p.26 Read the poem *Jump and Jiggle* on page 26 of the Companion.

Prepare to perform it, using your hands to show how each of the creatures moves.

Research it!

Favourite poets

p.18–31 Who are the poets whose poems you most enjoyed in this unit?

Can you find other poems by these poets in poetry anthologies in school?

Use the internet. See what you can find out about the poets. Make a mini-biography of each poet.

- ⊙ Are they still alive? If so, how old are they?
- ⊙ Where do they live?
- ⊙ What do they look like?
- ⊙ Do they have any family?
- ⊙ Why do they write poems?
- ⊙ Which poems do they like reading?
- ⊙ What kind of books do they like reading?

Sort it!

Waiting at the Window words

p.28 Read the poem *Waiting at the Window* on page 28 of the Companion.

List all the words and phrases from the poem which show the raindrops going slowly, and all those that show the raindrops going faster.

In your book, write:

Slowly	Fast
ooze	going pretty fast

Making sense of poems

p.28 Read the poems on page 28 of the Companion and the poem *Forth Went the Thunder-god* on the opposite page. Answer these questions in sentences.

Football at Playtime

1 Why do you think the game can't last for much longer?
2 Do you think they're playing in summer or winter? Why?
3 'Sticking their tongues out': what are the two different meanings for this phrase? Which one do you think the poet means?
4 Why is the narrator better off than Joe?
5 Why will Joe get the blame if they lose?

Waiting at the Window

1 Is the narrator a child or an adult? How do you know?
2 Is the narrator very busy? How do you know?
3 Have you ever played a game with yourself where you have said that if one thing happens then everything will be good and if the other happens then everything will be bad? Which lines in the poem suggest that this is the game in the poem?
4 What stops John from starting well?
5 What does 'I told you' in the last line tell you?

Forth Went the Thunder-god

This poem is meant to be a joke!
(Think about how the horse pronounces *th* to get the joke.)

1 What is the thunder-god's name?
2 What is a filly?
3 What did the filly think Thor had said? Why?
4 Why is forgetting a saddle a problem?
5 The author of this poem is 'Anon.' What does this mean?

Forth Went the Thunder-god

Forth went the thunder-god
Riding on his filly.
"I'm Thor," he cried.
His horse replied:
"You forgot your thaddle, thilly."

Anon.

Time travel

p.30 Read the poem *Talking Time-Travel Blues* on page 30 of the Companion.

Draw what life is like in the year 5000 for the time traveller, and what he or she hopes to find in the year he or she visits. Draw the time traveller too.

Unit 3 — Local History Detective

Enjoy it?

p.32–45 What did you think of unit 3, 'Local History Detective'? What did you find interesting?

Scan it!

Overview

p.32–45 Skim through unit 3, 'Local History Detective', to get a good idea of what it contains. Scan individual pages for information that interests you. What can you find out about your local area just from this activity?

Are there things you want to find out more about?

Do you know where to find more information? Try:

- your local library;
- your local newspaper – it may have a website;
- the internet.

Make notes about things you find out.

Adjectives

Adjectives have two main jobs. One is simply to describe. Another is to evaluate and give an opinion. Look at this list of adjectives. Write them in two columns.

big   old   new   easy   hot

colourful   great   beautiful   wet   important

fun   excellent   red   nice   dangerous

expensive   scary   fantastic   busy   calm

In your book, write:

Descriptive adjectives	Evaluative adjectives
big	great
red	fantastic

Newmarket clue quest

p.32–33 On pages 32 and 33 of the Companion, find:

1 what happened to the 'old market';
2 what the signs of a Georgian house are;
3 where the cock-fighting pit once was;
4 what the Devil's Dyke is;
5 who built the Devil's Dyke.

WELCOME TO NEWMARKET

Snap it!

Local photos

If you have access to a digital camera, try to take some photographs of places in your local area. Label the photographs and write captions to show what you can find out about the history and geography of the area from the photographs.

Join it!

Connectives

Different connectives join sentences in different ways. Choose a connective from the box to join each pair of sentences. Write the new sentence. You can only use each connective once!

Connectives	
after	but
although	however
and	so
as a result	then
because	therefore

1 I like living in my house. I'd rather live in a castle.
2 Town signs sometimes show historical people. They also show important events.
3 We don't always know what public art means. We can often work it out.
4 I have learned when the windows in my house were made. I know how old my house must be.
5 Making people feel proud of their town is important. They look after it better.
6 The Anglo-Saxons arrived in Britain. The Romans left.
7 People like erecting statues. They are expensive.
8 The Romans came to Britain. The Anglo-Saxons arrived.
9 My house is quite modern. It has big windows.
10 The Vikings lived in my village. It has a Viking name.

In your book, write:

1. I like living in my house but I'd rather live in a castle.
2.

p.36 **Read page 36 of the Companion. Which sentence summarises it best?**

A Streets are sometimes named after the local hospital.

B Streets are named after Dr Astley.

C Street names can tell us about important people and places from the past.

D Streets are given names for all kinds of different reasons.

E Streets are named after old places.

What's in a name?

p.37 **Use the information on page 37 of the Companion to think about:**

1 why most of the invaders and settlers didn't reach Scotland, Wales and Cornwall; why there are many more Celtic place names in these parts of the UK, and what this tells us about the Celts;

2 what kind of features invaders and settlers used when naming places. Were they mostly man-made or natural? Why?

Make a list of 20 different cities, towns and villages near where you live. What can you find out about settlers in your local area?

- ○ Main Roman towns and forts
- Anglo Saxon areas
- Viking areas
- Celtic areas

Draw it!

Make a map

p.37 Draw a map of an imaginary area in the UK. Label the places on your map using information on page 37 of the Companion. Write a brief description of the history of the area. Where in the UK would it be likely to be?

Reorder it!

Sentence sense

p.40–41 **Look at this sentence:**

Local stone has always been the cheapest.

Rewrite the sentence at least six times, reordering the words. Try to:

- make at least two sentences or questions which still make sense, but where changing the words around changes the meaning;
- make at least one sentence where you have to add a couple of words to keep the meaning;
- make at least two sentences which have the same words but which don't make sense.

In your book, write:

1. Has local stone always been the cheapest?
2.

Limestone quarry in Cumbria

Key ideas

Make notes of the key ideas in this passage. Use either a list or a diagram.

Many people in the UK live in suburbs on the outskirts of towns and cities. Suburbs are often cleaner to live in than city centres and have space for bigger houses and gardens. The suburbs in big cities have good transport into the city centres so that people can commute to work. There tend to be more houses than flats in the suburbs.

Although people like to live in city centres for convenience, housing is often very expensive there and houses tend to be smaller. Today, small houses near city centres that were built for Victorian factory workers are very popular, even though they don't usually have gardens.

In the UK today, 89% of people live in towns, cities and suburbs and only 11% live in villages or the countryside.

Happy endings

p.32–45 Finish each sentence using information from pages 32–45 of the Companion.

1 People build public art because …
2 We don't always know what ancient public art means, but …
3 We can often tell which invaders settled in an area because …
4 Sometimes streets are named after famous people; however …
5 Although front doors are the most important feature of a house, …

6 Victorians put coloured glass panels in their front doors in order to …
7 People in Britain didn't have glass windows until …
8 During the 18th century, some people bricked up their windows because …
9 In Tudor times, glass was very small to …
10 People have used local materials to build houses, nevertheless …

In your book, write:
1. People build public art because it shows pride in the community.
2.

House history

p.38–41 Look out of the classroom window. Can you see any houses?

Use the information on pages 38–41 of the Companion to find out when the houses were built and what they are made of.

Fill it out!

Hot and cold houses

Rewrite the notes below in two paragraphs of explanatory text.

Houses in different countries are built to keep the weather out.

balconies to provide shade

air conditioning

Hot countries

small windows to keep heat out

sloping roof to allow rain and snow to fall off

small windows to keep heat in

chimney – lets smoke out from the fire

Cold countries

stilts to raise the house up from the cold ground

Describe it!

Instant poem

Write an instant poem to describe your school – or an imaginary school:

In line 1 write the title	My school
In line 2: two adjectives	Cool, happy,
In line 3: an adjectival phrase	Ultra-modern
In line 4: a verb and an adverb	Progressing slowly.

The Industrial Revolution

What do you think of the Industrial Revolution?
Do you think it was good for people or bad
for them? Make a list of good things and bad
things you have found out. Discuss them in
your group. You could also make a poster.

spinning jenny

Use some of these facts about the Industrial Revolution in your debate or your poster.

⊙ For centuries, linen and wool had been spun and woven in cottages on farms in the country, but in 1733, John Kay invented the 'flying shuttle', which wove much faster, and in 1764 the 'spinning jenny' was invented. Now, one person using the machines could do as much work as 20 people without them.

⊙ Huge mills were built to house these big machines.

⊙ During the 18th century (1700–1799), steam engines were invented and improved until they could power whole factories.

⊙ People moved from the country to towns to find work in factories.

⊙ New factories were built on the edge of towns because that's where people were.

⊙ More factories were built in the north of England to be nearer the mines that were there.

⊙ Factories were built near rivers for water power and in order to transport coal and goods. Towns grew up around these factories.

⊙ Housing was built for the workers, who were very poor.

⊙ In the country, people had fresh air and could grow food, but in the slums the air was polluted by smoke, people had no fresh food and disease spread quickly.

Fantastic future

Sketch a 21st-century building.
Pretend you're the architect
and write a boastful poem
about it.

Hoozah Heaven
The Hoozah building is:
Taller than Mount Everest
Posher than caviar on smoked salmon
And more beautiful than the Milky Way.
Kate Ruttle

Unit 4 Moon Stones

Enjoy it?

p.46–59 Read through unit 4 of the Companion. Did you enjoy the story *Moon Stones*? Which bits did you especially like? Why?

Draw it!

Jupiter and Europa

p.48–50 Use the information on pages 48 and 50 of the Companion to draw and label a coloured diagram of Jupiter and Europa.

Write it!

Planet poem

Write a short poem about Europa, or the dome, using adjectival phrases. (Remember, poems don't have to rhyme.)

In your book, you could write:

Europa is as cold as ...
It is as icy as ...

Orbiting apostrophes

Rewrite these phrases, adding apostrophes if you need them.

1 Jupiter is in our Suns solar system.

2 Jupiter is made of liquids and gases.

3 Three of Jupiters moons are bigger than Earths moon.

4 Its possible to see Jupiter without a telescope.

5 You cant see Europa from Earth without a telescope.

6 Europas slightly smaller than Earths moon.

7 Its surface is covered in ice.

8 Cracks in Europas ice may have been caused by the pull of Jupiters gravity.

9 We couldnt breathe in Europas atmosphere.

10 Some planets dont have any moons; others have several.

Find it!

Future facts

p.46–59 **Find the evidence in the story *Moon Stones* that it is set in the future. Write today's equivalent for each piece of evidence.**

In your book, write:

Future	Today
1. book-pod	book
2. robo-pool	

Set it!

Alien landscape

Write a short setting for a story. Choose one of these landscapes, a building and at least one alien.

In your book, write an opening paragraph, which could begin like this:

Silence. Not a sound. Then Jeb's sensitive ears picked up a faint whisper. It sounded as if a fingernail was being scraped across a frozen lake.

Aliens

Landscapes

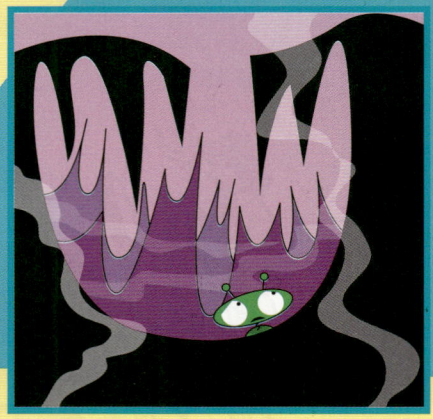

Buildings

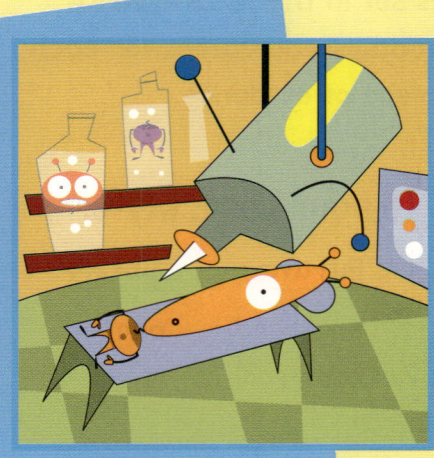

Label it!

Europa dome

p.47-53 Read the description of the dome in *Moon Stones*. Label the plan of the dome and its surroundings. Write something about each of the labels.

In your book, you could write:

1. building where everyone lives and works. Made out of ...

Three-part sentences

p.46-53 Write three-part sentences (sentences with three different bits of information) about Europa and the dome. Use information from these boxes or from the Companion.

The dome:

protective

broad

home

a scientific research station

high

made of special plastic

tough

moving

floating above the ice

floating on a cushion of power

Europa:

cold

icy

quite close to Jupiter

flat

some ridges on the surface

thin atmosphere

In your book, you could write:

1. The dome was high, broad and made of special plastic.
2.

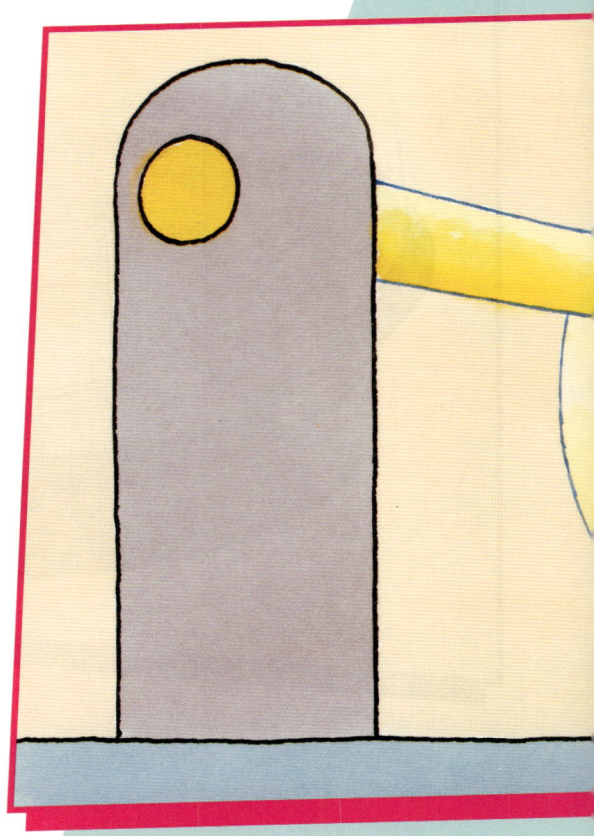

Explore senses through a freeze-frame

p.53–55 **In your group, reread chapter 3 of *Moon Stones* in the Companion. Ask one person to narrate the scene while the rest of you mime Dav's actions. Think about:**

◉ what you are thinking at this moment;

◉ how you feel;

◉ what you can see;

◉ what you can hear;

◉ whether you can taste or smell anything.

Narrator, break whenever something particularly interesting happens and call out the name of a member of the group. That person should freeze, while the rest continue to mime the story as you narrate. When all of the actors have frozen, think about how they are using all their senses, then take one of the positions so that one of the others can look at everyone else. Everyone in the group should have the chance to look at all the others.

Once you have all had a chance to look, find out how many of your senses the story described and how many you had to add to make each position.

Tape it!

Dome soundtrack

p.54 **When Dav stepped out of the dome, what sounds did he hear?**

◉ his own breathing?

◉ engines driving the dome?

◉ ice cracking?

◉ wind?

Use percussion instruments and other classroom sound effects (crumpling paper, rustling crisp packets, sharpening pencils, percussion using body parts, etc.) to make a filmic soundtrack to create a feeling of the planet.

Describe it!

Sci-fi similes

p.46–57 **Use a simile to explain how Dav felt at each point in the story *Moon Stones*.**

In your book, you might write:

1. When he first saw the blocks of ice, Dav felt as if he would explode with excitement.

1 When he first saw the blocks of ice, Dav felt as if …
2 Everyone laughed at Dav and he felt as if …
3 While he was waiting for the dome to reach the ice, Dav felt like …
4 When Dav knew that all of the children had had the dream, he felt as if …
5 When Dav heard the whispering, it sounded like …
6 When Dav got out of his bed, he was moving like …
7 Dav's scream was like …
8 Dav clambered up the ice blocks like …
9 The ice that formed around Dav was like …
10 When Dav heard what the aliens said, he felt as if …

Act it!

Hot seat Dav

p.46–57 **One person in your group should be Dav from the story *Moon Stones*. The rest of you can think of questions to ask 'him'. They might include:**

- Did you like living in the dome *before* you found the ice blocks?
- Why do you want to be a space scientist when you grow up?
- What made you think the ice blocks were put there by aliens?
- What did you feel when everyone laughed at you about the aliens?
- Why didn't you insist on telling your mum about the children's dreams?
- Why didn't you shout out when you were being pulled by the alien force?
- How did you feel when you were trapped in the ice block?
- What exactly did you say to Jeni when you were trapped in the ice block?
- Why do you want to be there when the aliens in the ice blocks wake up?

Finish it!

Moon endings

p.46–57 **Finish each of these sentences, using ideas from the story *Moon Stones* in unit 4.**

In your book, you might write:

1. Dav and his mother lived in the dome because Dav's mother was a scientist on Europa.

2.

1 Dav and his mother lived in the dome because …
2 Dav was nearly eleven so …
3 The planet Jupiter almost filled the sky because …
4 Dav really wanted to meet an alien but …
5 After Dav had the dream, he …
6 Dav thought that the ice blocks might have been placed there; however …
7 Alind teased Dav about his belief in aliens, and furthermore he …
8 Dav listened to the whispery voices, and as a result …
9 Finally, Dav made the scientists listen, and consequently …
10 Although Dav was only eleven, he …

Screen setting

Think of one of your favourite films – it could be a cartoon, adventure story, western, historical story, romance ...

Each action scene in a film is filmed with its own 'set' or background.

Draw or write a description of a film set or background — either one you have seen, or one you have made up — and briefly describe how the characters would behave in it.

In your book, you might write something like this:

Setting: A cartoon forest with signs on all the trees asking people to hand over all the fairy tale characters they know. The forest is spiky and unwelcoming with dark colours and lots of shadows.

Characters: People are pulling in fairy tale characters who all look depressed and are painted in dull, dirty colours. The people are all wearing black and grey. Everybody is cross and miserable.

Review it!

Short story

Choose any short story you have enjoyed. Write a recommendation to persuade other children in your class to read the story. In your recommendation, include information about:

- ◉ title;
- ◉ author;
- ◉ setting;
- ◉ characters;
- ◉ brief description of the story (but stop at the climax – don't tell us how it resolves itself!).

In your book, you might write:

Title: The Three Billy Goats Gruff
Author: unknown
Setting: meadows, a mountain, a bridge and a stream

Unit 5
Cinderella Stories

Enjoy it?

p.60-79 Read through unit 5 of the Companion, thinking about all the different Cinderella stories. Which is your favourite? Why?

Think it!

Cinderella's Britain

At about the time the version of the story we call *Cinderella* was first written down:

- King Charles II was king of Britain;
- people didn't often travel, but when they did, they travelled by foot, by horse or by carriage;
- the Great Plague killed people throughout London (1665);
- the Great Fire of London swept through London (1666), after which Sir Christopher Wren began to build St Paul's Cathedral (1675);
- the first dinosaur bones were found (1677);
- the first gas-powered street lamps were being erected (1681);
- the composer J. S. Bach was born (1685).

Can you think of features in the Cinderella story you know which are historic?

How would the story have to change if it was being told in today's times?

What can you find out about the times the other stories were written in?

Say it

Tell it!

Cinderella's story

As a group, prepare to retell the story of Cinderella. Plan and rehearse, so that you all know exactly what you're saying and everybody is telling the same story.

Think it

Listen to it!

Soundtrack to Cinderella

Listen to some music by Bach, Handel or Vivaldi, all of whom were writing music about 300 years ago.

As you listen to the music, think about how people would have moved and danced to it.

This was the kind of music Cinderella and the prince would have danced to.

Sort it!

Famous fairy tale tellers

p.63 Find out who first wrote down these fairy tales.

Group the tales into sets by the author(s), then see if you can find similar themes in each set.

Themes could include:

Puss in Boots

The Little Mermaid

Thumbelina

Little Red Riding Hood

The Emperor's New Clothes

Sleeping Beauty

Rapunzel

The Ugly Duckling

Hansel and Gretel

Cinderella

hope   cleverness   cruelty

magic   overcoming hardship

change   trickery   revenge

courage   goodness   injustice

In your book, write:

Author:	Themes
Stories	

Fairy tale fiction and fact

In 1981, Prince Charles, heir to the British throne, married Lady Diana Spencer.

This was said to be a 'fairy tale wedding'.

Why do you think it might have been called this?

Match it!

Match the marks

Match the punctuation mark to the name and description.

In your book, write:

Punctuation mark	Name	Description
.	full stop	marks the ...

.   ,   ;   :   —   " "   ?   !

comma

speech marks

exclamation mark

full stop

semi-colon

dash

question mark

colon

- ⊙ marks the end of a question
- ⊙ separates ideas in a sentence
- ⊙ show the words someone says
- ⊙ marks the end of a sentence
- ⊙ introduces a list of ideas
- ⊙ marks the end of an exclamation
- ⊙ separates closely related sentences
- ⊙ used in informal writing to replace other sentence punctuation

Rhodopis

p.66–67 Read the story of Rhodopis on pages 66 and 67 of the Companion. Decide which of these sentences is the best summary of each paragraph.

In your book, write:

Para 1: Rhodopis...

Paragraph 1

Ⓐ Rhodopis was Greek.

Ⓑ Rhodopis was gathering seashells.

Ⓒ Rhodopis was captured and sent to be a slave.

Paragraph 2

Ⓐ At last, Rhodopis began to feel better.

Ⓑ None of the other slaves liked Rhodopis.

Ⓒ Rhodopis began to make friends with the birds and animals.

Paragraph 3

Ⓐ Rhodopis met a falcon.

Ⓑ The master gave Rhodopis some red shoes.

Ⓒ Rhodopis' master saw her dancing.

Paragraph 4

Ⓐ Rhodopis was left behind while the other slaves went to see the Pharaoh.

Ⓑ Rhodopis had to grind the grain.

Ⓒ The other slaves gave Rhodopis even more work to do.

Paragraph 5

Ⓐ Rhodopis waved goodbye to all the others.

Ⓑ The falcon, who was the god Horus, took one of Rhodopis' shoes.

Ⓒ Rhodopis was sad.

Paragraph 6

Write your own summary of this paragraph. You can use two sentences!

Write it!

Traditional story challenge

Can you rewrite a traditional story in no more than 100 words? You must include all the usual traditional tale details in the story and you must write in full sentences.

Compare it!

Same and different

p.62 **p.70–73** Read the old story of Cinderella on page 62 of the Companion and the modern one on pages 70–73. In your group, make a list of things which are the same and things which are different in the stories. Think about:

- the people;
- the story theme;
- the events;
- the objects;
- the beginning;
- the ending.

Find it!

Cindy

p.70–73 People are described in different ways in the story. Who is the author talking about when she writes:

- the spiteful sisters?
- DIY mechanic?
- the sulky sisters?
- the FGM?
- fitness fanatic?
- trendy dancing girl?
- dear Miss?

Sentence type transformation

Transform each of these sentences into a different sentence type.

1 Are you charming enough to be a prince? *(transform into a statement)*
2 Marry the first girl you see! *(transform into a negative)*
3 Don't dance with one girl all night. *(transform into a question)*
4 If someone treads on your toe, stamp on theirs. *(transform into a negative)*
5 You need to think about what you want to do. *(transform into an instruction)*
6 Do you need to take a break? *(transform into a statement)*
7 Be kind to all the girls! *(transform into a statement)*
8 You are a modern man. *(transform into a question)*
9 Smile! *(transform into a question)*
10 Will you marry Cinderella? *(transform into a negative)*

In your book, write:

1. You are charming enough to be a prince.
2.

Fairy tale fill-up

p.60–79 Use the Companion to write answers to these questions in sentences.

Non-fiction

1 When and where was the first story of Cinderella thought to have been told? **p.61**
2 Why do you think many traditional stories are about poor people? **p.60**
3 Did the Brothers Grimm invent their stories? **p.63**
4 What kind of weapons were British people fighting with when the Chinese invented gunpowder? **p.65**
5 What was drawn on Tutankhamen's sandals? **p.67**

6 Why don't people nowadays wear the same make-up as Queen Elizabeth I did? **p.74**
7 What did men in the 17th century wear that men don't usually wear these days? **p.74**
8 What is the difference between dreaming of Prince Charming and waving a magic wand? **p.76**
9 'Quit stressing' is informal language. Why is it used on this page? **p.77**
10 Why do you think the princes in the different stories would have been skilled with different weapons and would have hunted different animals? **p.79**

Fiction

1 What were the insults the sisters used in the Grimm Brothers' story of Cinderella? **p.63**
2 In the Perrault story, why was Cinderella given her name? **p.62**
3 Why did Yeh-Shen have to get her slipper back when she lost it? **p.65**
4 What happened to Yeh-Shen when she put her second slipper back on again? **p.65**
5 How do we know that Rhodopis lived near the sea in Greece? **p.66**

6 What made the other slaves dislike Rhodopis? **p.66**
7 What made Rhodopis' master very sad? **p.67**
8 Why did the old woman tell Chinye to take the smallest gourd? **p.69**
9 Why did Adanma care that her cowrie shells were destroyed? **p.69**
10 What is 'new-found wealth'? **p.69**

Write it!

Character portrait

Write a character portrait of one of the characters from any story in unit 5 of the Companion. In your portrait you should include:

- what she/he looks like;
- what his/her hobbies are;
- his/her favourite food;
- his/her likes and dislikes;
- what she/he thinks is important.

Some of the information is in the stories – but some of it, you'll have to make up! Use your knowledge of the stories to think of likely answers.

Enjoy it?

p.80-93 Read unit 6 of the Companion. Where would you most like to go? Why?

Draw it!

Alien illustrations

p.80-81 Look at the descriptions of the aliens and their planets on pages 80 and 81 of the Companion. Draw your idea of one of them (it doesn't have to be the same as the illustrator's idea). Label your picture to show which details from the description you have used.

Split it!

Alien syllable split

Read the names of each of the aliens. Can you pronounce them? Split them into syllables to make them easier to read. Write the syllables.

In your book, write:

1. Barf – a – min – its
2.

Can you write the names of the capital cities in the unit like this, too?

Who's saying what?

p.80–81 Use the information on pages 80 and 81 of the Companion to work out which alien's saying what.

Ah! Bliss! What is better than floating gently with a warm sea slug and a fingerful of salt? This is just what I need after a hard day's swimming.

1

Today is my best kind of day because it has been raining all day long. The sun nearly peeped through the clouds, but luckily a good, thick black cloud came along just in time to cover it up. Just as well, because I can't enjoy a good mound of mould if it's sunny!

2

Harrumph! Would you believe it? I had just found the best tortoise of the day when my friend (well – I used to think it was my friend, but I will never talk to it again!), just sucked it up! Just like that, without so much as a please!

3

I was in the Big Cave today when suddenly a breeze flew up and wafted me back home again. I was a bit unhappy because I wasn't yet ready to come home. But what can you do?

4

Have you ever been to Slugalug? If not, you should go there. Most of all, you should go to Café Slugsville because they have the best snotflies ever. You may think you have eaten good snotflies, but wait until you see them there!

5

I have a problem because one of my wheels is loose. I don't know how it happened, but look! Now I can't even get to the drive-in, although luckily my dad is going in so he'll bring me a pizza.

6

Find it!

Connectives 1

Read the alien speeches above.
Which connectives can you find in them?

Remember – connectives are used to join ideas. You can find them in the middle of a sentence (*I was cold* **so** *I went home*) or at the beginning of a sentence (**Now**, *I am at home*).

In your book, write:

because, but, ...

Connectives 2

p.80-93 Search for connectives in unit 6, 'Alien Travel Agency'.
As you find them, list them in two columns to show where you found them.
Try to find at least five different connectives for each column.

In your book, write:

Within a sentence	At the beginning of a sentence
and	well

Say it

Musical punctuation

Read the poem opposite in pairs.

Think of a sound you could make to show each of the different punctuation marks. Practise performing the poem, with one of you reading the words aloud and the other making punctuation sounds.

To make the different sounds, you could use:

- patting, clapping and stamping;
- whistling, clicking and singing;
- a variety of percussion instruments.

Search it out!

Meaning of marks

Choose a double page spread from unit 6 of the Companion. Make a list of the punctuation marks you can find. Then explain why they were used.

In your book, write:

full stop – used at the end of a sentence

comma –

On Some Other Planet

On some other planet,
near some other star,
there's a music-loving alien
who has a green estate car.

On some other planet,
on some far distant world,
there's a bright, sunny garden
where a cat lies curled.

On some other planet,
a trillion miles away,
there are parks and beaches
where the young aliens play.

On some other planet,
in another time zone,
there are intelligent beings
who feel very much alone.

On some other planet,
one that we can't see,
there must be one person
who's a duplicate of me!

John Rice

Language games

Write a brief description of each of these things.

Then, write a sentence to persuade someone to buy it.

Example:

1. An apple is a crunchy fruit.
   Eat an apple! Crunch your way to health!

Discuss your sentences with a partner.

How are your sentences different?

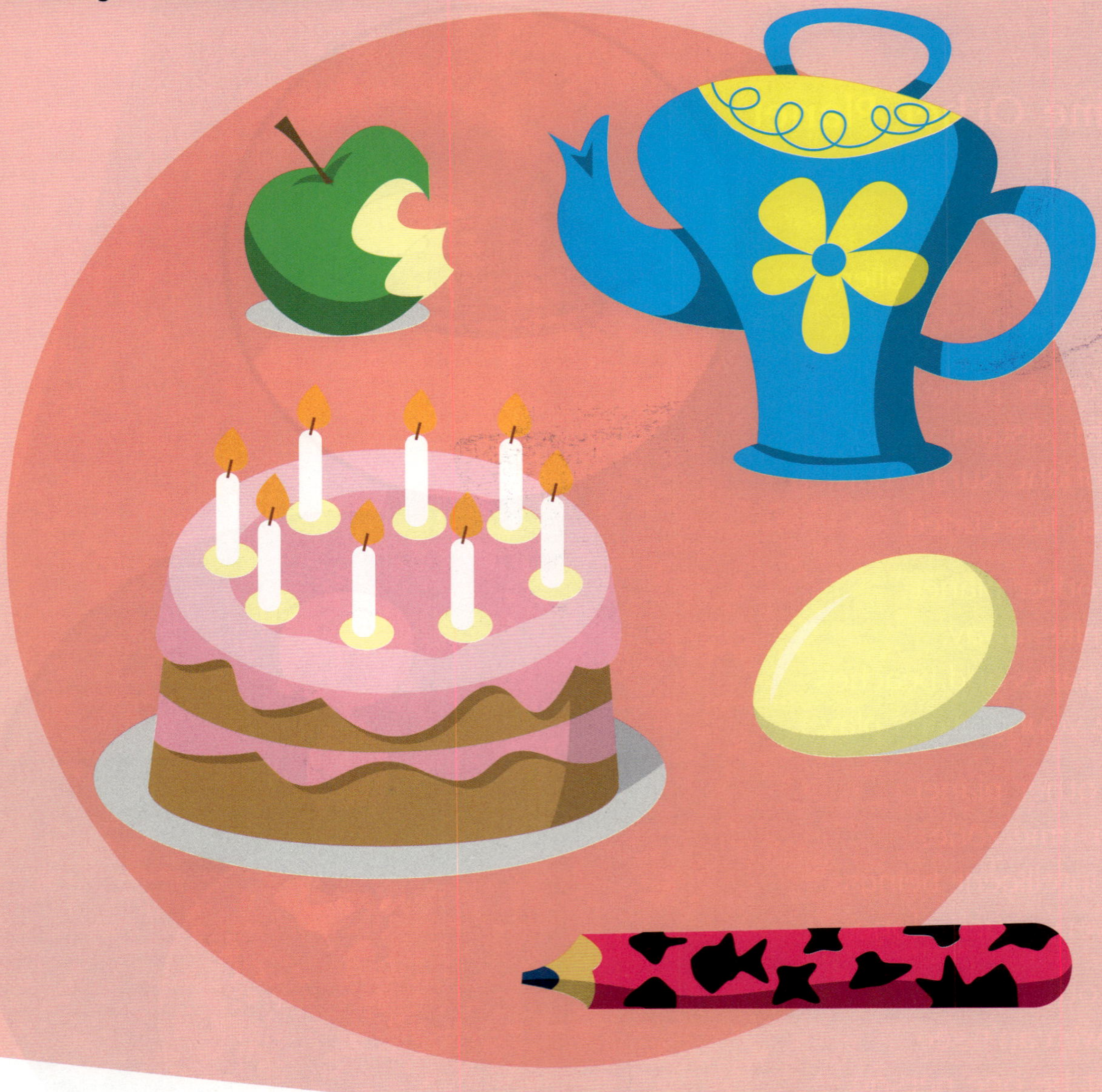

Make it!

Adding endings to words

p.84 All of these words are on page 84 of the Companion.
Try adding the endings in the circle to each sets of words.

Now, write which sets of words each ending can be added to.

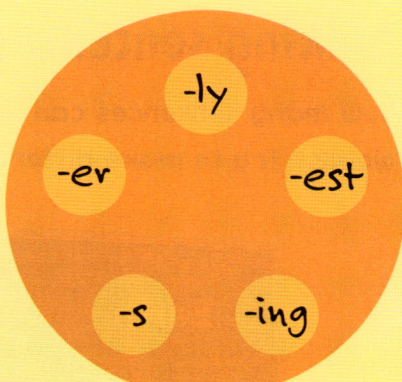

-ly
-er
-est
-s
-ing

In your book, write:

'-ly' can be added to adjectives.
'-est' can be added to …

Nouns	Verbs	Adjectives	Others
rainforest	pour	dark	with
page	live	sunny	above
home	make	warm	next
cat	cut	damp	below
tree	look	bright	the

Think it!

Changing words

Choose a double page spread from unit 6 of the Companion. How many different word endings, or suffixes, can you find? Make a list of them and see if you can work out what kinds of words they can be added to.

Are there any prefixes on the pages? What kinds of words are they added to?

Order it!

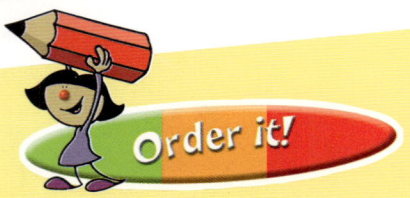

Making sentences

How many sentences can you make using each set of words? Try to make different sentence types each time.

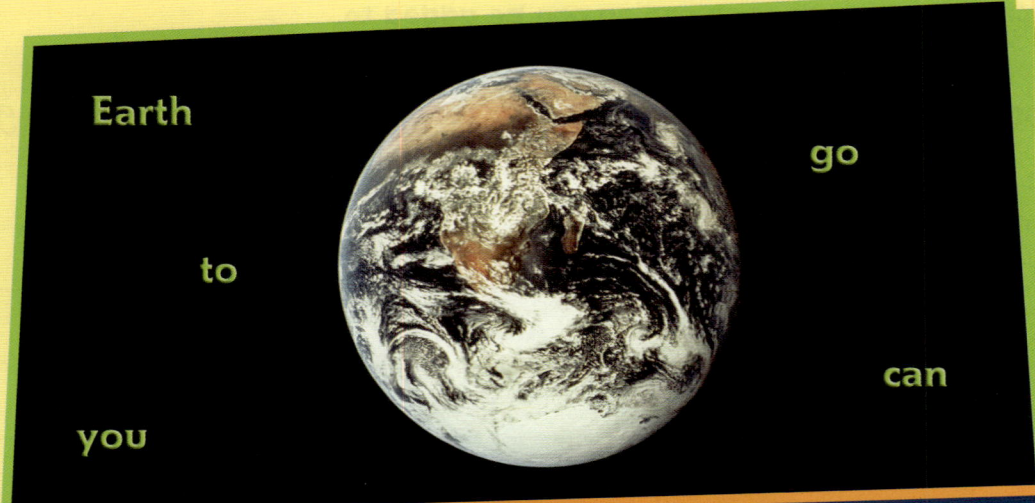

Earth
go
to
can
you

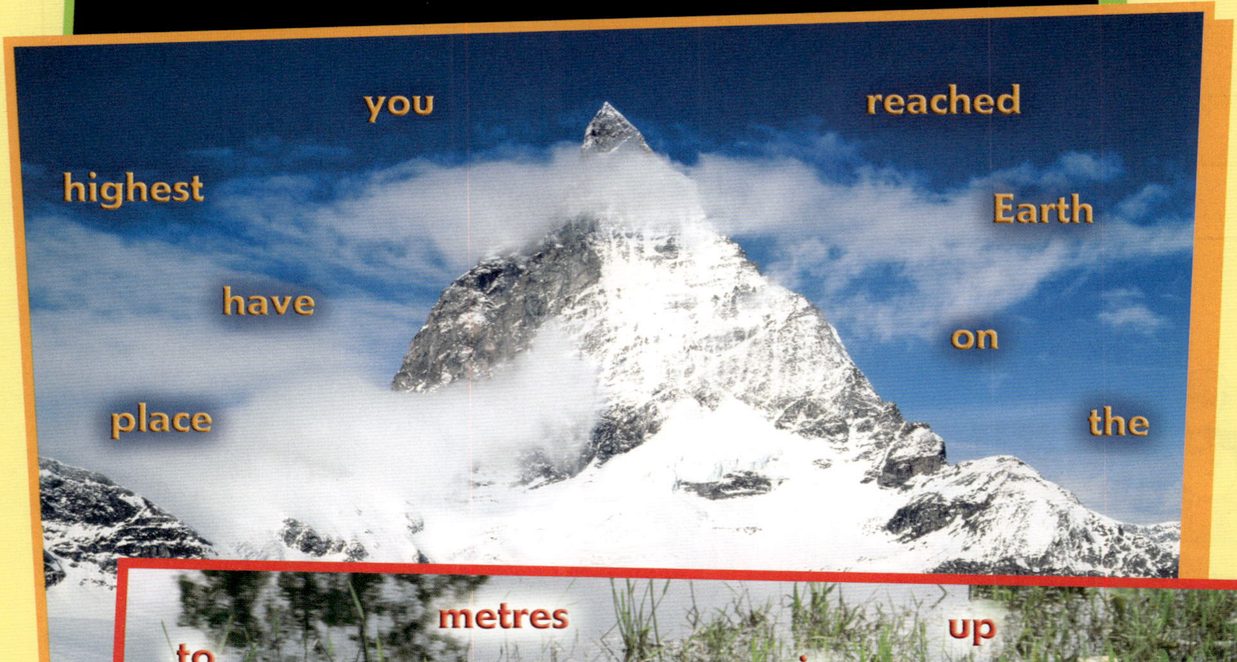
you
reached
highest
Earth
have
on
place
the

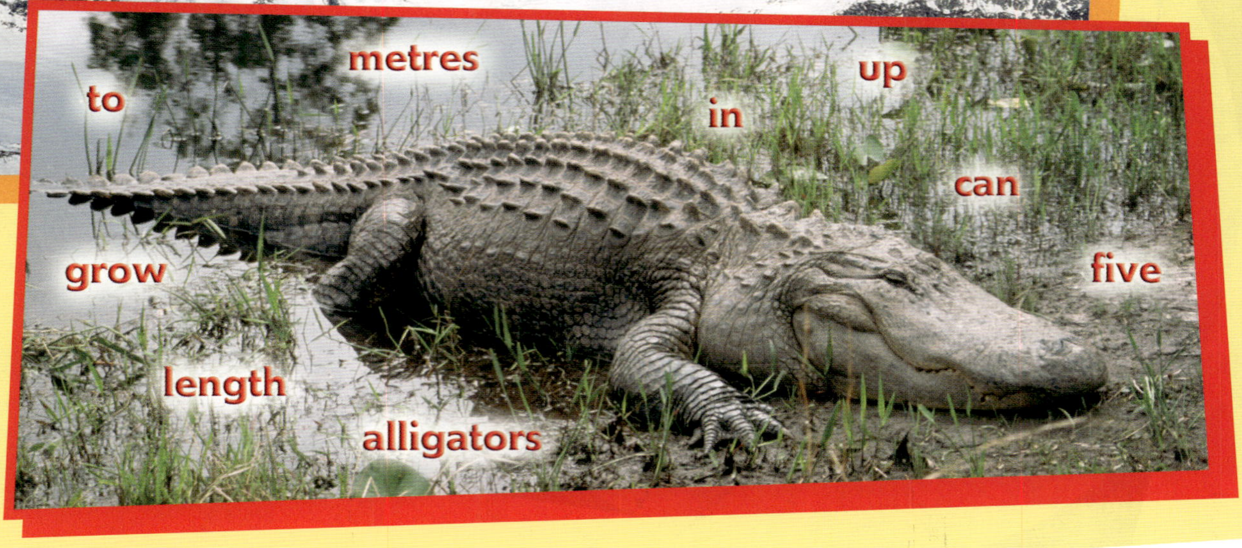
metres
to
up
in
can
grow
five
length
alligators

Evaluating author's words

p.84–89 Read the description below. Which other words could the author have chosen instead of the underlined words? Look at what the author is describing and discuss why you think he chose the words he did.

1 a rip-roaring, radical <u>roller-coaster ride</u> of really incredible opposites **p.84**
2 <u>massively</u> tall trees **p.84**
3 big cats, like the <u>deadly</u> jaguar **p.84**
4 the <u>amazing, stupendous</u> banks of beautiful, colourful coral **p.86**

5 the <u>incredible</u> marine life **p.86**
6 a <u>perfect</u> place for underwater exploration **p.86**
7 you've really reached the <u>heights</u> of holiday fun **p.87**
8 Can you <u>beat</u> the fear inside you? **p.87**
9 The Himalayas – <u>only for heroes</u>. **p.87**
10 The Autobahn is just <u>made for speed</u>. **p.89**
11 something <u>blurs</u> past you in the lane outside you **p.89**
12 You like <u>life in the fast lane</u>, so the Autobahn's the place to be. **p.89**

Be prepared to talk about your answers with a partner.

Transforming sentences

Read these sentences, then reorder the words to make the sentence type shown in the table. You might need to add words or leave them out.

Original sentence	Change to a ...
1. The Reef is home to the deadly lionfish.	question
2. Do bottlenose dolphins play by the Reef?	statement
3. There are six species of sea turtle.	question
4. Did you know that the Reef can be seen from space?	statement
5. Go to the Great Barrier Reef.	question
6. Did you read about the Great Barrier Reef?	command
7. There are 2000 kinds of sea creature near the Reef.	question
8. Are there whales near the Reef?	statement

Argument connectives

Read this argument about the best holiday for Murmuroids. List all the connectives you can find.

Caves are the best place on Earth for Murmuroids to have the holiday of a lifetime.

The Mammoth Cave National Park is a network of caves which are ideal for Murmuroids. Families can enjoy a home-from-home holiday because there is room for all, although some members of a family might be asked to share one of the roomier caves. However, the joys of a cave holiday will make this seem unimportant.

Murmuroids will enjoy the peace inside the caves, especially in the deepest caves which Earthlings never reach. Moreover, you can meet new animals which also hate noise and light, and swap ideas for decorating caves. They have some wonderful cave decorations! In addition to all of this, the caves are dark, dank and cold. Mammoth Cave is ideal for the Murmuroid who wants to travel, without having to try any new experiences.

List it!

Caves for Murmuroids

Using the passage above, and what you know about Murmuroids from the Companion, write a list of the main points to support the argument that Mammoth Cave is the best place on Earth for Murmuroids to have the holiday of a lifetime.

Alien connective collection

Think of a different connective to join each pair of sentences. Write the new sentence each time.

Replace it!

Think of two different connectives to join each pair of sentences. Write the new sentence each time.

1 Kanga-bangas might want to go to Brazil. They may prefer the Galapagos Islands.

2 Kanga-bangas like eating tortoises. They might like marine iguanas too.

3 Barfaminits will enjoy the Barrier Reef. They will find sea slugs there.

4 Barfaminits might enjoy the Barrier Reef. They might not like Mount Everest.

5 Tads might want a holiday on the Autobahn. They might not.

6 Who would win the fight? A Tad met an alligator.

7 Caves are ideal for Murmuroids. Caves are like their homes.

8 Murmuroids could go to the Sahara Desert. It is quite unlike their home.

Act it!

How do they move?

p.80–93 Imagine you are one of the aliens from the Companion on holiday. How would you move around? What would you do? You can't speak any Earth language, but do you have your own language made up of sounds or movements?

Prepare your movements and sounds. Can other children guess which alien you are and where you are on holiday?

All about Earth

p.84–91 Use information in the Companion to find out where ...

1 bottlenose dolphins live;

2 eyeless crayfish live;

3 you can ride a 'ship of the desert';

4 apple snails live;

5 you can be blinded by dazzling headlights;

6 egrets wade;

7 to watch out for the alligator;

8 to find Annapurna;

9 Irukandji jellyfish live;

10 to find the blue-footed booby.

Amazing alien

Think of a new alien. What does it look like? Where does it live? Where on Earth would it like to go on holiday?

Draw your alien.

Make a table like the ones on pages 80–81 of the Companion to give information about your alien.

Write down key ideas about somewhere on Earth your alien might like to go on holiday.

Writing mat

Key features of some useful text types

REPORTS

Purpose: to describe the way things are

Structure:
- open with a general statement
- paragraphs begin with topic sentences
- headings and subheadings organise information
- non-chronological

Language:
- present tense (unless it's a historical report)

Writing tips:
- gather interesting and memorable information
- use tables and diagrams to add new information
- you can use questions as sub-headings for each paragraph

EXPLANATIONS

Purpose: to explain a process or how something works.

Structure:
- begins with a general statement
- a series of logical steps explaining how or why something occurs

Language:
- usually present tense
- connectives that show cause and effect
- sequencing connectives

Writing tips:
- use flow diagrams if they are helpful
- use the words *how* or *why* in the title
- use the first paragraph to introduce your subject to your reader
- think about whether or not you need to include a glossary

INSTRUCTIONS

Purpose: to tell the reader how to do something

Structure:
- opens with a goal
- lists materials needed
- sequenced steps to achieve the goal
- numbers or arrows to show order of steps

Language:
- command verbs in second person
- adverbs show order of steps

Writing tips:
- think of ways to interest your reader
- use adjectives and adverbs only when they are necessary
- If your reader doesn't already know what to do, will these instructions help?

PERSUASION

Purpose: to convince the reader to do or think something

Structure:
- opening statement introduces topic
- arguments why you should do or believe it
- ends with a summary and restatement of the topic

Language:
- present tense
- often second person
- cause and effect connectives

Writing tips:
- address your reader directly
- be informative, but friendly and persuasive
- use facts as well as persuasive descriptions
- make your language memorable